WEAVING EMOTIONS

A JOURNEY TO SELF - EXPLORATION

AN UNINHIBITED SAPIENT

This book is a deeply personal exploration of my journey through emotions, growth, and self-discovery. The stories and reflections shared are a representation of my truth, as seen through my own experiences and feelings. It is not my intention to cast blame, criticize, or harm anyone mentioned in this work. The people and events referenced are significant to my personal development, but this book should not be interpreted as an objective account of any individual's actions or character. Rather, it focuses on my perceptions, emotional responses, and the lessons I have learned. I recognize that others involved may have different perspectives or memories, and I deeply respect that each person has their own truth. My goal is to foster empathy, healing, and understanding for those who may identify with my experiences. If you recognize yourself in these pages, I hope you find a new appreciation for the impact you have had on my journey. Above all, this book is meant to Inspire readers to reflect on their own paths of growth and transformation, and I offer it with the hope that my story will resonate in a way that promotes healing and connection.

CONTENTS

ABOUT THE AUTHOR

As a 23-year-old wordsmith, my heart skips a beat for the world of words, driven by a quest for self-discovery. Having journeyed from a place of giving up on life to embracing my future self, I can truly say that I haven't just aged — I have been through every moment of it.

Today, I'm thrilled to carve out my space and nurture resilience. Through my odyssey, I've learned to celebrate my individuality and trust my authentic self. In reclaiming my fragmented psyche, I define my essence as:

Little at heart,

Older by thought,

The same red runs in me, too !

And apparently, have I been looked upon as human…

But do I even, or will I ever, fit in ?

I'm hopeful to be one someday,

So here I am, on the journey !

To make some space, and build a home for me.

For learning is a journey,

that transcends eternity.

So I've needed to provide myself a space :

To learn, then unlearn, and to relearn.

22/6/24

My debut book, "Weaving Emotions: A Journey to Self-Exploration" a poetry-memoir hybrid, is a testament to the transformative power of hope and self-awareness. The twenty-one initial verses in it narrate the pivotal event that changed the course of my life—an unexpected boon that emerged from the darkness.

With a writing style that blends lyrical prose and raw honesty, I invite readers to immerse themselves in my journey. This collection is a tribute to the human spirit, a celebration of the resilience that lies within us all.

I'm deeply grateful to the supportive spirits who championed my cause, cheered me on, and inspired me to hold the pen with renewed courage. Their selflessness is something I will forever admire.

I hope you'll join me on this journey, and trust that you will find resonance as we explore the complexities of life, hope, and self-discovery together. Also, your active engagement would be my greatest reward !

HEARTY READING !

MY TAPESTRY TO THEM

Here, I offer my heartiest tribute to all those who radiated their generosity with their kindest hearts, providing me solace and comfort that nourished my soul in ways I couldn't have found on my own.

They ? They who ?

All of my closest friends, who, together with me, sailed us safely from the wrenching days of early twenty.

All of my honorary elderly lights, who considerately inspired me to hold on to hope with their positive affirmations.

All the passers-by, who inspired me with their genuine kindness, leaving a lasting impression on the existence of humanity !

Together, they all

Helped me connect the blocks to pave a rock-solid path, where I am paddling ahead with a resilient spirit.

And above all heights, to my **late grandmother**, who never failed to inspire me with her wisdom and generosity through all her ever-loving embraces.

To a pair of incredibly supportive parents, who selflessly nurture me.

And **my only sibling**, who's been distant but has never failed to be my rock throughout my journey.

It's never enough to just convey my gratitude or feel grateful , but I can only bow down to them with all my heart and offer them a prayer for their well-being until eternity.

As a way of conveying my gratitude to them all, I wrote a verse, which I've included below -

I WAS PLEASED !

I was pleased !

I was pleased !

If someday I'm ever asked :

"Hey ! When was the time you felt most heard ?"

I would heartily say :

Every time I approached those genuine hearts,

Every time I was vocal to them,

Every time I wanted to be seen,

They ignited me with a light

that had been absent during my darkest hours.

Every time I needed clarity,

they would come up with vivid options in a row.

With time, such blessings of theirs have become

one of my most prized assets :

and my favorite invisible jewel,

which adds more moral gravity within me.

Hence, such blessings of theirs nourish my soul

to resume life comfortably.

23/12/23

Considering all of them my friends, I felt an irresistible inner call to give voice to their impact on me and the lessons I've learned from them. What better day could I choose to communicate my message to them? But on Friendship Day! So, I jotted down :

If ever, by way of any event, our paths have crossed and we could interact,

If ever, we had clicked on one another and felt a connection,

If ever, we were able to exchange our ideas,

If ever, I could keep my words to you for the reason that I felt at home in you,

If ever, you thought of ringing me up because you could connect with me without hesitation,

If ever, you could believe that I was capable of your trust,

If ever, we could release our shoulders on each other,

If ever, you significantly impacted me,

You are the one to whom I'll always remain obliged.

The inspiring one ! By the effect of whom:

I could continue to soldier on,

I could address myself with a kindness I never knew existed,

I could learn the essentials of social interaction,

I could recognize the power of human bond,

I could understand the reasons for the acceptance needed to thrive within a social setting,

I could learn that being different is another definition of being unique,

I could realize the essentiality of putting one's shoulder to the wheel,

I could learn that there resides an invisible battle behind a decent smile,

I could learn the potentiality of having enough mental strength,

I could know that holding oneself accountable for all that we do is indeed an indispensable requirement,

I could realize that we all are in the making of our individual processes...

And for the last to this day,

I could finally learn that :

We have all met because of the choices we made.

And now, we are all paving our way,

Casting around for our homes…

~ And with this little arrangement,

Here, my heart irresistibly goes out to say—

HAPPY FRIENDSHIP DAY !

18/7/24

UPON LIFTING THE VEIL

I never thought I'd find joy in holding a pen, nor did I ever feel a particular quest towards the world of words. But upon composing my first verse in 9th grade (2015) as a class assignment, I remember searching for words that would rhyme and convey my intention. To my surprise, I managed to maintain the rhyming symmetry throughout the verse. The thrill of capturing my eleven-years journey of school in rhyming words ignited a spark within me.

Despite struggling academically, I gradually found solace in writing. However, it wasn't until 2021 that I discovered my true calling. A moment of external validation electrified me, and I began to find reason in everything. From then on, *writing* became a way to express my emotions and a source of pleasure. The turning point came when a renowned teacher praised my way with words, awakening me to my own ability.

In the first quarter of 2022, inspired by that honorary teacher, I tried to ink my words for a national occasion. As the year passed and as I entered 2023, I was consumed by a thought reclaiming myself from my earlier experiences, which caused me to explore the idea of 'Reciprocity'. I then poured out my thoughts and inked them as my third verse. This concept appears as ' Reciprocity that leads' -the very first verse in the pages you will read.

Thus, I began writing my initial verses without rational thought, never imagining that I would develop an unrelenting interest in delving into this craft.

Right after that, I couldn't think of any new ideas to explore. However, after a gap of several months, it was my grandmother's love and resilience that inspired me to pick up the pen again. I remember the day she was lying helplessly in bed, when her fracture prevented her from walking. I was consumed by sadness, thinking she wouldn't be able to spend time with me actively, that our walks and moments together would be a thing of the past.

I then wrote my fourth verse, "One More Year !" where I poured out my emotions as I struggled to come to terms with this new reality:

ONE MORE YEAR !

Whom do I ask for another year ?

A year:

Where we would cook our favorite meals together...

One more year:

Where we would dance to our favorite song...

One more year:

Where we would rant about family matters...

One more year:
Where we would enjoy our three meals together...

One more year:

Where we would talk about random things and end up bickering...

One more year:

Where we would have deep conversations about our family...

One more year:

Where you would advise me on how to be a perfect daughter against all anger...

One more year:

Where you would guide me to weave correctly...

One more year:

So that we can truly celebrate each day together...

One more year:

Because you deserve it.

One more year..

One more year...

One more year....

July 27, 2023

It was July 2023, when by a way of accident inside the roof, she suffered a mild fracture. Now, to hope for further recovery from such an advanced age had its own inherent risks and challenges. Her full recovery seemed nearly impossible. None of us, nor she, was affirmative about it. I saw her lying in discomfort, struggling with the pain of the fracture in a difficult-to-diagnose area of that tiny body. It was in that moment of struggle that these thoughts waved in my head, and somehow, I tried to pick up the pen…

Although, there have been gaps in my writing journey, the urge to continue has become organic. By 2024, I've been fortunate enough to find my purpose in writing, which brings me immense joy. I'm grateful for that initial spark, my grandmother's love, and the encouragement that followed. Today, I feel utterly blessed and at ease, to have discovered my voice and passion.

WHISPERS OF MY GUIDING ANGEL: A JOURNEY OF RENEWAL AND TRANSFORMATION

Finding reasons to live with a contented heart often felt beyond my grasp, weighed down by emotions I couldn't fully understand or control. From the day I became aware of my mind, I recognized an inner fragility— core insecurities and negative thoughts that flowed through me beyond my control. This inner fragility often manifested in my behavior; for instance, whenever I became angry, especially towards my grandmother, it led to disrespectful actions. I later realized this was because I lacked a fully developed empathetic heart, a deficiency that seemed to be either inborn or a consequence of my surroundings. My social insecurity and lack of confidence made it difficult for me to interact and engage as others did, further isolating me and intensifying my sense of being adrift without guidance.

Over time, these unrelenting thoughts led to unresolved negative emotions, which in turn drove me toward behaviors I later regretted, leaving me consumed by guilt. I longed for a confidant, a presence who would listen without judgment and offer me hope that I, too, could be a person of worth. But without that, I was left adrift, with no sign of blue.

This sense of being lost was further complicated by my upbringing, shaped by the discord that filled our home. The tension between my caregivers' conflicting views and values created a toxic atmosphere, making their relationship my everyday concern. I felt trapped and helpless, unable to escape the emotional turmoil that weighed me down. Their fractured relationship cast a long shadow over my childhood and made it hard for me to find joy in life, leaving me feeling like I was merely existing, burdened by constant pain and distress. The weight of their struggles was so overwhelming that I sometimes questioned the value of my own life.

As a result, from toddlerhood to my teenage years, I struggled to unlearn the rigid parameters of my upbringing. This attitude of being preoccupied with insecurities persisted throughout school, college, and into my bachelor's degree. But I never imagined that a spontaneous decision to attend a college, which would later become a turning point in my life, would alter my journey. In 2019, I enrolled with renewed determination after a lackluster performance in my higher secondary exams. While the college itself wasn't a catalyst for change, the experiences and encounters I had during my time there set me on a new path.

The first half of my bachelor's program went smoothly, but due to a regional political crisis, our exams were delayed until late December 2019. After the exams, I returned home for vacation, and everything seemed normal until January 31, 2020. On that day, I was struck by a severe chill just as I was about to leave for my paying guest room to start the second semester. The cold was unbearable, forcing me to cancel my plans. Over the next few days, my condition became more severe—I developed a severe headache, high fever, persistent cough, distorted taste, nasal bleeding, and severe fatigue. Despite these symptoms, I attended classes, but my health kept declining. My parents noticed swelling in my upper eyelids, which worsened each day, leaving me irritated. Concerned, they sought medical help in a major city, but none of the doctors could diagnose my condition.

As my health deteriorated, my brother took me to a renowned hospital in a distant city. His courage and determination got us there. By the time we arrived, my muscles were so weak that I had to use a wheelchair. Unable to eat and feeling my body giving up, my brother's care was crucial during this harsh period. We Placed our trust in the doctors, who conducted a series of tests. The test results revealed that I had Systemic Lupus Erythematosus (SLE) — an alien concept to my family and me. It is an autoimmune disease that attacks healthy tissues, causing inflammation and damage to various organs in the body. In my case, SLE led to nephritis, affecting my kidneys, and pancytopenia, reducing my blood cells. The diagnosis was a turning point, marking the beginning of a new journey. Grateful for my parents' unwavering support, who relentlessly backed my brother's decision and selflessly provided all the necessary financial resources for my treatment, and my brother's willpower, I received the necessary treatment. Their unconditional love and presence helped bring me comfort and peace of mind during those difficult time. This was further enhanced by the exceptional care of my doctor, who has been instrumental in my care since the beginning and continues to be a guiding light to this day. His exceptional expertise and compassionate approach make me feel secure, worry less, and remain hopeful for a bright future. Since my diagnosis, under his expert guidance, my disease has been in remission, and I am living normally.

After my diagnosis, my treatment had just begun, and we returned home shortly thereafter. During those days, I struggled to imagine walking normally as the disease took hold. With semester exams approaching, I feared having to drop out. Fortunately, the COVID-19 pandemic led to lockdowns, which aligned with my situation and spared me from a gap year.

As I continued treatments, my condition stabilized, though I experienced significant physical and hormonal changes. By the time colleges reopened, I had made significant improvement and was ready for a fresh start. The lockdowns and online classes provided an unexpected benefit by giving me the time I needed to heal and adjust, which played a crucial role in my recovery.

While embarking on this new path of managing my health, I felt prepared to embrace new challenges and found myself at a crossroads where my physical recovery began to intersect with my emotional and psychological healing. During this transitional phase, everyday actions and interactions around me began to hold new significance. Though not intentionally designed to support me, these experiences felt profoundly uplifting and played a crucial role in altering my outlook.

With offline classes resuming, I found myself entering the final year of my bachelor's program, marking a new phase in my journey. We were required to do a fieldwork related to our course. During that departmental fieldwork trip, something within me shifted. The positivity of our teachers throughout the trip, including their encouragement to sing and dance during the bus journey, along with the exciting spirits of my friends who joined in, inspired me to embrace a more hopeful and open attitude.

And on our return, I vividly remember enjoying a moment entirely new to me—standing in the bus with my classmates, singing and dancing with full spirit. It was the first time I felt I could live with a soaring spirit. That experience planted a seed of hope, making me believe that I was finally breaking free from the rigid confines that had long kept me from truly living.

Later, on an ordinary day, while exploring with friends, a chance encounter with an artist brought a significant shift. When approached with a request for a portrait, the interaction was marked by an exceptional blend of artistry and genuine kindness. Their genuine interest in capturing me on canvas resonated deeply within me, helping to counterbalance my self-doubt and bolster my sense of self. This unexpected moment, combined with the meaningful collection of photographs, became a source of external validation during a time when fragile confidence and insecurity, heightened by the physical changes from my treatment, were my constant companions. The encounter offered a glimpse into a kind of humanity and creativity that felt both inspiring and uplifting. It added a significant boost to my journey, laying the foundation for a path enriched with newfound hope and possibility.

This experience lifted my spirit and reinforced my path forward. I had always wanted to express my gratitude to those who supported me during my health battle, yet I was searching for the right way to do so. The sense of upliftment infused me with so much courage and positivity that I felt ready to start my social media handle, creating my first video as a heartfelt dedication to those who helped me along the way.

It was through that video that I reconnected with a significant figure from my past, someone who had been a guiding light during a transformative phase of my journey. Sharing the video with them, I was filled with anticipation, and their response exceeded my expectations. They praised my writing and the personal growth I had achieved since we last connected, leaving me feeling elated—like I was on cloud nine.

This person had always been a source of wisdom and inspiration for me, particularly during a time when I was grappling with my inner struggles. Their encouragement during those early years had a lasting impact on how I viewed myself and my path forward. Their natural way of speaking made me feel at ease once more, and I realized that their presence in my life was far from over.

What made this reconnection even more meaningful was that they understood the emotional landscape I was navigating. Having faced similar challenges in their life, they offered me insights that I had been searching for but hadn't found anywhere else. I began to see them not only as a mentor but as a bridge to a deeper understanding of myself—helping me unravel parts of my identity that I had long struggled to reconcile. Our conversations opened doors to aspects of my life that had been left untouched for years. I found myself reflecting on how far I had come and how much further I could still go, with their guidance lighting the way once more. Meeting this impactful individual seemed to change perspectives those which were deeply rooted within me. Their warmth and encouragement planted a seed of hope in me, making me feel like I was finally connecting with someone who could guide me in the way I had always longed for.

Overwhelmed with excitement, I eagerly began sharing more of myself with them, and that marked the beginning of our conversations. Though I was shy at first because of my admiration for them, I was also overjoyed to be forming a connection with someone I found so inspiring. What made them truly remarkable wasn't just their perseverance, but the way they transformed their struggles into opportunities for growth. Despite facing numerous setbacks that could have easily derailed their path, they carried on with unwavering determination. Each challenge became a stepping stone, allowing them to redefine their sense of purpose and resilience.

Their strength didn't come from external validation but from within—a quiet, steady force that pushed them forward when others might have faltered. They found meaning not in the absence of hardship but in their ability to navigate it, emerging on the other side with greater clarity and self-assurance.

This version emphasizes the **internal resilience** and **personal transformation** of the character, shifting the focus away from loss and toward their ability to grow through adversity.

As we grew closer, I began to sense that they were quietly struggling with something. Even though they never spoke about it directly, I could feel their unspoken burden through our conversations. This combination of my admiration for them, the connection we shared, their kind treatment of me, and the empathy I felt for their hidden suffering—something I could sense but not fully understand—stirred something deep within me and made me want to help them. Without even knowing the cause of their pain, my care for them deepened. In my desire to support them through whatever they were going through, I found myself falling deeply for them as I came to understand their intentions toward me.

Although I was motivated with a sense of purpose after a long battle with self-doubt and had decided to face the upcoming challenges with undivided attention, I found myself increasingly distracted. I was uplifted by all the validations from those around me, which made me feel so worthy that I initially decided against forming any new personal connections and instead chose to focus solely on my academics. Despite this commitment, I found myself unexpectedly drawn toward the individual who seemed to offer deeper understanding and support. Their influential presence profoundly affected me—familiar yet distant, with a blue aura that resonated deeply within me.

Unbeknownst to me at the time, there was a yearning within—a longing for a deeper connection. What struck me even more upon reconnecting with this person was how their character and demeanour, which I had admired in the past, still left an indelible mark on me, resonating deeply with the unfulfilled aspects of my own journey.

Despite facing their own challenges, they exuded a remarkable sense of empathy and grace. Their ability to handle difficult situations with calmness and humility was a breath of fresh air, a stark contrast to the harsh patriarchal dynamics I grew up with, where the family head's dominance and control often left the female figure feeling belittled and silenced.

Though our time together was brief, the way they conducted themselves made a profound impression. I admired their genuine concern for others and their ability to navigate complexities with ease. This experience made me reflect on how fortunate someone would be to share a life with such a thoughtful and compassionate individual.

When I reconnected with them through that video and began to share more of myself, I recall with vivid clarity the day they spoke about our first meeting. They described me with a level of detail that seemed almost reverent—mentioning the flowing cascade of my hair and a distinctive feature on my face as if these were unforgettable impressions from that moment. It was as though they had captured the essence of me from the very beginning. Additionally, their feedback on my creative expression in the video was incredibly validating, consistently highlighting my strengths and insight in a way that made me feel truly seen and understood. This was combined with their constructive appraisals, which further emphasized my writing abilities and made me feel valued.

With each deep conversation we shared, my admiration for them grew. As I discovered more of their inner world, I witnessed their natural empathy, generosity, simplicity, and loyalty. Interacting with them became a mirror, helping me better understand my own emotions and needs. Their qualities, along with the conversations we shared, prompted introspection and clarity, helping me navigate my own thoughts and feelings more deeply. The way they stimulated me intellectually made me realize that I could feel at home with them—a safe, comfortable home full of purity. Our conversations would flow so naturally that time seemed to slip away. Sharing more of myself with them became second nature, something I had never experienced before. I had never found such deep comfort in talking to someone; it felt as if I had finally encountered a kindred spirit.

Though we never explicitly discussed love, we connected deeply through everyday topics. I would share my concerns with my friends, and they too would share their own experiences. We found common ground in our mutual interest in cooking, as we both loved experimenting in the kitchen. Their profound sense of humour was another fascinating feature I admired; they could find humour in the most tense situations, a trait I had always wished to experience but never found in my family or elsewhere. Unlike the frustrations and complaints I was used to, their ability to approach challenges with a light-hearted perspective was a breath of fresh air—a lateral thinker indeed, and someone I felt I truly wanted to be with.

There was an unspoken bond that felt as though their heart was craving to express something, yet remained unspoken. It was the first time in my life that I had encountered such a profound connection with anyone. They shared that they felt comfortable talking with me, as if I were their own. I, too, felt an extraordinary connection, as if I had found my soulmate—someone whose presence aligned so closely with mine. Our conversations felt miraculous, centered on our individual lives without any hint of distraction. Initially, my feelings stemmed from admiration, but over time, it became clear that they too recognized our budding connection.

What stood out even more was the way their nature and wholesomeness touched me in ways I hadn't anticipated. Unknowingly, they met hidden needs I hadn't been aware of. I never thought that simple conversations could offer so much comfort, to the point where I began to admire them deeply. At times, I recognized parts of myself reflected in their character. The way we communicated made it feel as if both our inner selves were at ease, allowing for a natural closeness. I could open up my entire being with them, as if they were a shoulder to lean on without hesitation or fear of judgment; on the contrary, they nurtured every bit of me in an admiring way. Not only did they offer appreciation, but they also provided rational, thoughtful criticism, which I valued. It made me feel as though I could grow alongside them.

Interestingly, I had never sought out a partner or entertained the idea of one. In fact, I had firmly decided not to pursue such things. But this connection felt different. Another significant factor was how naturally they seemed to fit into my life, as if everything would fall into place without effort. This made me start envisioning the possibility of a future together. As we grew closer, they once said, "The one who calls you theirs will be eternally grateful." These words were unexpectedly touching, making it all the more gratifying to know that my feelings were reciprocated.

Considering my journey up to this point, I recall how the visual artist's validating gesture lifted me during my period of self-rejection and how high I felt as I emerged from shadows to prominence. This newfound confidence was further nurtured by the profound positive influence of the impactful individual, whose comforting presence made it challenging for me to let them slip from my thoughts. As a budding soul, I wholeheartedly believed in the wisdom my tender senses gleaned from their words and I had put my trust on them. During that transformative period, their platonic words became crucial in soothing my tender heart in ways I hadn't anticipated.

Yet, amidst the comfort, a nagging sense lingered. Although I wasn't certain, I felt something wasn't aligning with my perception. As they gradually created distance, I couldn't quite pinpoint what felt off, but the feeling persisted. With limited time due to academics, I struggled to understand my mental state while being in their presence. I became so absorbed in the comfort they provided that I failed to realize my role was meant to be merely temporary.

When I finally confronted the truth behind their seemingly gentle façade, my world crumbled. The realization that a future together was unattainable was a harsh reality to accept, leaving me emotionally unsettled and devastated. I was thrust into a harrowing phase of turmoil and confusion. At that time, struggling to understand why they were stepping back from being close to me, I couldn't directly ask them, as I didn't want to make them feel disrespected or burden them with accusations. I had to keep my feelings suppressed, and during that time, I found myself forming several assumptions: 'Maybe they're withdrawing because they're afraid to get too close due to the struggles they face in life.' This very thought caused me immense pain. I was almost broken. There were days I would cry… cry and cry… grieving endlessly until exhaustion took over. I was utterly shattered, a feeling I had never experienced before, causing extreme pain within my tender heart. As much as I felt at ease with them, the detachment was a heartache I had never felt before. It was as if I was experiencing heartbreak for the first time—an agonizing pain that made me fully understand what it feels like to lose someone you deeply longed for. The torment of having to part from someone with whom I had envisioned a future and with whom I had woven so many dreams was overwhelming, leaving me to wrestle with an excruciating, internal anguish.

Only after understanding their true situation did I realize that the space I had considered a temporary refuge was not as it seemed. This revelation forced me to let go and continue on my path, but the emotional impact of separation left me deeply unsettled and torn.

On the other hand, with the mounting academic pressures of final semester, I needed to recover and bounce back quickly. In that moment, it was the individual's soul-validating words that helped me navigate through the emotional turbulence stirred by our interaction, they were the one to rationalize things for me in the most moral way possible, bringing solace to my shattered dreams. The fate they revealed although contrasted to my notion of perceiving them, but their thought-provoking moral words helped me to learn from them and inspired me to overcome my harrowing emotional breakdown. It did take a huge toll on my mental energy to get through the situation, but with the consolations of my closest ones, I was somehow able to return to a sense of normalcy.

Later on, conversations with them about their early experiences helped me develop a rational understanding of how to navigate social settings. This, in turn, enabled me to bridge the gap between the rigid constraints of my childhood and the newfound freedom I was discovering. I was beginning to shed the irrational insecurities that had held me back—insecurities stemming from my upbringing, where I had struggled with self-doubt due to average academic performance and a lack of confidence in my social appearance. Embracing this freedom allowed me to adopt a more positive and open attitude, moving beyond the limitations that once constrained me. The process of unlearning the constraints of my early years became essential in embracing the person I was evolving into.

Amidst the academic demands, my confidence was shaken, and self-doubt came uninvited, affecting my wellbeing and undermining my sense of self— aspects I have delved into further in the section entitled "A Journey Through Turmoil And Redemption."

Those self-doubts plagued me for months, pushing me to the brink of giving up. Supported by those closest to me, I recovered, though healing took time. Just when I was about to get back on track, something awe-inspiring happened, which I have described in more detail within the same section : immediate cure and closure came through the impactful individuals offering profound words of affirmation. Their reinforcement, arriving at just the right moment, healed the mental ailment I never thought I would recover from. Their words, serendipitous and unaware of my condition, provided ultimate relief. The joy of relief from my self-imposed cage was immense. I felt transformed and renewed. They restored all the BLUE to me, acting as a remedy. Their profound impact helped me discover a bluebird within myself, with whom I have fallen in love ever since. For me, blue represents the serenity and tranquillity that their presence brought into my life, symbolizing the calmness and peace I had been searching for but couldn't find until our paths crossed. Their presence and words brought clarity and comfort to my soul, reminding me that hope and healing are always within reach. This feeling of sincerity and hope serves as a constant reminder of the deep sense of tranquillity and emotional healing that emerged from our connection.

As I look back, I see how profoundly my experience with this person has shaped my perspective. Despite the hardships they faced, their character and resilience left a significant mark on me. The way they navigated their life, relying on their own inner strength and wisdom, enriched my understanding of personal growth and self-discovery.

What stood out was their genuine interest in me, which made a lasting impression despite the complexities surrounding our connection. This genuine attention, despite the circumstances, led me to reassess my self-worth in a new light. It suggested that perhaps there was something of value within me that they could see, and this realization was both enlightening and humbling, altering my self-perception and encouraging me to value myself in ways I hadn't before.

Their philosophies and insights, shaped by their personal experiences, provided me with a fresh perspective on life and emotional connections. Through their practical help and thoughtful advice, they revealed a deeper understanding of how these connections function in reality. When I shared my feelings for them, they gently clarified that what I thought I was experiencing was actually admiration. This new insight helped me see the distinction between admiration and deeper emotional bonds, shaping my understanding of emotional connections with a more practical outlook.

Though my feelings were unreciprocated, the impact they had on me has been profound. Their influence helped me reshape my approach to life and relationships, highlighting the importance of self-awareness and emotional intelligence. This journey of admiration and reflection continues to inspire and guide my personal growth.

As I continue to reflect, I realize that particular interactions and gestures led me to perceive them in a certain light, suggesting a special affection or deeper interest from my side. Their way of talking to me, comforting me, and showing empathy made me feel seen and understood, which in turn stimulated my own affection for them and created a connection on my end that I hadn't initially anticipated. Without these moments, my perception of them might have been different.

Yet, despite this misunderstanding, the impact they had on me was undeniably transformative.

Now, as I revisit the steps of my transformation, it becomes clear that it was the power of this angelic individual that helped me emerge from the darkness and struggle. Thus, they transformed from a source of past torment into my soul's saviour, illuminating a path toward healing and redemption. Their influence made me admire them as if they were from a metaphorical heaven, with a heavenly aura that profoundly impacted me, helping me feel whole again.

What more can I say about this angelic presence and our transformative interaction? My hands always rest on my heart even while I think of them. It's a gentle reminder of the profound connection we shared, and the impact they had on my life. They played a remarkable role in finding and installing solace within my nest. I believe this solace will last within me forever, cultivating hope at every step until eternity. Therefore, the individual will always be remembered as the most ideal presence in my story, who provided a sense of belonging and hope that transformed my deeply rooted self-doubts into renewed strength. Their influence helped me see beyond immediate struggles and embrace a future filled with hope and possibility.

In summary, our brief time together had a profound and lasting impact on me. Their presence served as a lifeline during a later period of great uncertainty, and their overall role was highly significant in shaping my whole being. The resonance of their influence still echoes within me, leaving an indelible mark and reinforcing my path forward.

Thus, by looking back on this transformative experience, I present to you the first 21 verses of my debut collection, a poetic journey that captures the essence of my time with the individual. Each verse weaves together fragments of our encounter, from the initial meeting to developing an emotional connection, and then the eventual parting. These poetic echoes of our moments together, forever altered my path. I hope you'll feel their intensity, and sincerity as you read them.

UNFOLDING WHISPERS

As I reflect on my journey, I could address myself that, my personal experiences uncovered deeper truths about my own emotions. These emotions which were seeded from my encounter with the significant individual, have been explored intensely throughout the initial eleven verses I have inked here in. By channelizing my emotions and expressing every bit of them, I needed to hush the sighs of my soul, and they eventually became my muted whispers. Thus, 'Unfolding Whispers' represent this profound exploration and revelation.

After reflecting and channelizing my emotional baggage, I could somehow draw some insights from my personal experience with the individual. Now, as I present you with a tapestry of threaded emotions—each carefully woven in sequence— you will witness the stages of how the exploration of themes deepens, reflecting an evolving journey from fleeting moments of my connection with the individual, to the more profound introspections of longing and the passage of time. Thus, by delving into these poems, you will be able to explore the complexities of my unvoiced desires and the delicate balance between hope and resignation.

RECIPROCITY THAT LEADS !

For winter, to wrap up in a pullover,

Spring would process into rejuvenation.

Pretty summer would appreciate sleeveless attire, florals, shorts, and insect veils all together!

Autumn rehearses summer's heat while preparing for the winter dryness to come.

This is how they live (probably) and help life survive.

Now, as we adjust or adapt,

Is it just enough to wrap and unwrap our protections?

"What if their hopes are beyond our bars?"

"What if they would add modifications if you and I did a little more justification…?"

19/1/23

My encounter with the individual left an everlasting spark within me. Yet, after our conversation, I sensed a deep struggle in them—an invisible burden that seemed impossible to cure, yet had to be endured. As time passed, I grappled with understanding the turmoil within me. While I had no clear understanding of their pain, my emotions continued to stir, compelling me to write and seek the truth. I began weaving together an assumed cause: 'Perhaps, due to dissatisfaction, the individual feels lost today, starving like an infant deprived of their mother's warmth.' There was a weight in the air, a tension that suggested their unspoken pain and inner conflict. As I learned more about their past struggles, my empathy for them deepened. With their wholesome personality, I began to admire them, believing they deserved all the happiness life could offer. It felt unjust that they should continue living in pain, as if the life they were enduring wasn't truly theirs. These thoughts heightened my empathy and drove me to seek ways to provide comfort. Though I knew little of the specifics, I felt an urgent need to ease the turmoil I sensed. This compassion and desire to soothe unvoiced suffering led me to write—a poem inspired by my wish to understand them and my hope for their healing.

With this thought, I aimed to highlight the role of reciprocity, both in nature and human life. The seasons became a metaphor for this individual and their experiences. Each one reflects a different aspect of their emotional state, influenced by the subtle dynamics of their environment. Just as the natural world can be altered by human actions, so too can one's inner world be affected by external circumstances or missed opportunities. Through the lens of reciprocity, I sought to illustrate their distress, the silent compromises they've made, and the unfulfilled longing that now seems to shape their suffering. Their pain, I believe, stems from a missed chance or an opportunity that once held promise but has now faded away.

The "you" in this poem, though unnamed, subtly points to the forces or circumstances that may have failed to meet their expectations or aspirations. And just as imbalance in nature can lead to disruption, the absence of fulfilment or opportunity has left a void in their life. Yet, the poem carries an underlying message : just as negative actions can disrupt the natural balance, positive actions can contribute to healing and comfort. It also carries a hope : that by becoming aware of the small ways we impact others, by making even slight changes, we might restore balance, offering the possibility of healing where it is most needed. Thus, the poem reflects the idea of reciprocal relationship emphasizing that through understanding and compassionate reciprocity, we might to ease the burdens we sense in others, even if they are left unspoken.

Here you have the second verse, about my experience with the individual. Entitled "The Room I Read," the room here represents the individual's energy, as there were many instances where they weren't explicit but were subconsciously vocal about themselves. Believing that the soul of the individual deserves to seek all the blue they wish to be with, I subtly poured out my thoughts. The poem narrates how I felt completely invited by their warming words but was left with ambiguity about myself when they revealed a truth I hadn't previously understood and explained that my perception of them was mistaken. It highlights how I found my way to them and the aftermath of our encounter. Even after knowing the fate, my heart remains in denial, refusing to accept that whatever I sensed and read was wrong. The conviction I felt in that room was so intense that my heart kept whispering: I read them all right, and that the 'room' too deserves to seek solace wherever their heart feels invited and at home.

Towards the end, words flow to bring out the transiency of the individual and the fact that I needed to surrender myself to their fleeting nature.

So, for the reason, the last line goes –

For it all began when I read the room, which I wish I hadn't read, as I underwent days of struggle to embrace their transiency and accept my submission to the truth they were holding behind.

THE ROOM I READ

I found reading rooms to be more convincing in actuality than the words themselves.

For words uttered are presentably genuine ,

but they convinced me to disbelieve what I read and claimed it to be illusionary.

It denied being vocal, yet I could read it all !

Not knowing the reason for its interest fulfilment, I had to step out of it.

Now, the interest factor of theirs is again driven and has fair reasons to see hope – even in the darkest corners in the darkest corners where their heart finds it resonating with all the BLUE they could ever wish to be with.

But the room I read was fair, I believe !

Where breaking the ice was never a task, but pure intimacy !

Everything was so convincing, as if it were a season, and I kept falling every time I read them…

I know, it's just a matter of season and me !

A truth for real, but a dream unfulfilled in actuality !

For it all began when I read the room…

So, for that reason, I wish now—

If only 'reading room' was less convincing.

17/12/23

Having read the room, I was driven to cloud nine once and multiple times every time I entered. But after facing the truth, I had no other option but to let my soul surrender to it. However, being compelled to surrender couldn't help me convince myself to disbelieve the immeasurable comfort the room offered me. Failing to do so, I then had to allow myself to feel on 'cloud nine,' even if it was crystallized to be not mine.

Thus, the verse—entitled "A Gloomy Cloud Nine"—reflects the promise of experiencing cloud nine, even though it will inevitably succumb to gloomy weather.

A GLOOMY CLOUD NINE

Even if it is less convincing !

Even if it feels like a trouble undefined !

Even if it is crystallized to be not mine !

It feels irresistible on this side to be not on "CLOUD NINE !"

20/12/23

The irresistibility of forbidding myself from reaching cloud nine left a gloomy ache in me with each attempt. Reflecting on the transiency of seasons, I realized that using them as a metaphor could define the individual. The seasons symbolize their impermanence, mirroring the brief duration they offer.

Since it all began on a winter day, so goes the verse:

It all began in the apricity of winter, where the warmth of the season provided me with solace and new hope with every step, much like how spring symbolizes new beginnings. Their hopes made me feel secure even during the monsoon rains, which I didn't realize could signal a shift towards autumn. Blindfolded by hope, I failed to notice the rain's true sign until it ended, leaving me to fall like autumn leaves. Thus, the verse flows with a narrative that captures my journey with the individual through these seasonal metaphors.

SEASON AND I

Seasons are to live for, and so did I.

It all began in the apricity of winter,

They then walked with me like Spring !

We danced together under the monsoon rain -

I thought rain wasn't always a sign of bad ;

but soon their presence faded, and I fell like those leaves in autumn…

24/12/23

REFLECTION ON MY WITHDRAWAL

I know, in time to come,

We will be marching parallelly...

And there won't be a waterfall of seamless conversations

Between you and me...

But I will climb the rocks,

And long to flow with you...!

If you ever revisit my place ~ Did I withdraw?

25/12/23

Needing to surrender to the transience of the individual, my once preoccupied thoughts now linger in the air, as I sit still with a distorted rose In hand, holding onto an uncertain hope for a chance encounter. The swirl of events inside my mind leaves me doubtful, questioning: Did I withdraw, or am I still willing to remain, holding their memories close, and address the obscurity?

APOLOGETIC

My whims and desires are perhaps

"The Same Old Story"

to you...

But I'm on the moon !

Inscribing everything that was left to my imagination...

Every day, on a fresh page.

~ pardon me

26/12/23

My unmeasured exchanges with the individual left me ambivalent. At times, I would pull myself out, while many times, I would drift to the moon. This confusion deepened as I realized their presence in my life might not be possible. Holding onto the ambiguities made me fragile, allowing my half-filled whims to flow over the paper. As the comfort lingered within my soul, I was powerless to prevent it and allowed it to envelop me every other day, spreading across a fresh page of my memoir. Also, my meeting with them was an event that provided me with the never-before-experienced comfort. So, even after my surrender, I would continue to connect with my inner call and weave a new tapestry of emotion every other day, with the 'Same Old Story'...

A wish to address my language to the individual stemmed from the preoccupied thoughts in me, of a longing that couldn't be fulfilled. Later, this same wish led me to bottle my thoughts as a means of reflecting on my submission to the unfortunate circumstances that kept us apart, helping me to reconcile my role as a mere passer-by in their life. Thereby, acknowledging the unbridgeable distance between us.

Now, by the role of a passer-by, I tried to bring out the fact that I cannot have any legacy upon the individual but can still be a little while companion and offer a warm prayer to them:

A prayer that would ensure that they doesn't get lonely in their journey,

A prayer full of aspirations, and a prayer that would assist them to continue to march forward.

But having an extra bowl of offerings, I, as a passer-by, wanted to convey more than just a prayer. So, to express my heart, I have tried to wipe off all the dust from their path towards the end of the verse. The aura of the individual, which serves as a source of infinite joy for me, is indeed resembled by 'the most colourful path,' which is being projected as a dream of many other passers-by like me—those who hold them in high regard, whether as a dear friend or a cherished presence.

BEING A PASSER-BY TO YOU

What more can a passer-by convey :

but warmth !

A warmth that would serve you as a guiding lamp to see all the paths untaken.

What more can a passer-by convey :

but a prayer !

A prayer that would give you clarity to keep faith in yourself first, so that you pass the test.

Now, this passer-by has more to convey :

Not just to convey,

But to wipe off all the cloudy aura that is causing a vision blurry to the most colourful path, which every passer-by wishes to visit.

~ beholden…

9/1/24

__If__ you ever find my language,
I hope it speaks to you !

I hope you connect to my verse and find yourself.

And I hope you find not just a verse,

but a voice unmuted !

~ rosy

9/1/24

Consumed by the thought of a possible revisit
by the individual, I was left with a 'rosy' heart,
that if not through any real encounter,
I still would wish for it to happen through a fated
encounter. If that occurs, they will be addressed
with my language and will sense the voice through the
profound intent woven by my soul. By addressing this,
I further wish that the individual find their lost self and
recognize their true existence by unmuting my voice.

The verse' Being A Passer-by To You' denotes how, even after reconciling with fate , I continue to hope to offer my prayers to the individual. For which, I have chosen my role as a mere passer-by in their life. Apart from my wish to offer prayers, there had always been an inner call of gratitude and reverence on my end for them, who is resembled by 'the adored guest' herein.

So in the beginning, you read, how by a chance encounter I met the individual. You have also read , how the eventualities offered me a chance to cultivate resilience, and embrace whatever serendipity I was offered by way of our shared platonic aura. Who eventually became my BLUES with all the BLUE. For it is a bygone STORY, which I have sung aloud in the previous verses to honour the individuals role - whom my heart defines as the most adored guest in my journey until now, and I was so pleased to GREET them. How would I not, as it has been the most blissful event that has happened to me to date.

So by representing the individual as a 'Guest,' I am addressing a question—one that I might encounter in the future, or even if not outwardly, would still serve as an introspective conversation. This would guide my inner soul towards acknowledging who they are truly to me.

As the verse unfolds to describe my thoughts by responding to :

Who is the GUEST to me, and how are we related ?

With boundless exhilaration and fondness for them, I place my hands on my heart and let my voice rise:

MY ADORED GUEST !

So if someday, I'm ever asked :

"Who you are to me ? And what connection do we hold ?"

With blushful aflame,

a constant smile,

and keeping my hands on my heart,

I will tell them :

My heart defines you as the most Adored Guest of mine.

Who visited my place with a BOOKEY,

that had not just roses with thorns,

but prettiest flowers from all the seasons !

With whom,

I now hold a connection, that speaks volumes to my soul !

18/1/24

The roses here are metaphors for the temporary hopes I was wrapped in, depicted as thorny to symbolize it's fleeting and painful nature. Yet, like rose remains the queen of flowers despite its thorns, so does the GUEST remain cherished to me. From whom, I could rationalize myself with all the ethical values they had within—prettiest flowers from all the seasons are metaphors for all the morals the GUEST transmitted to me.

So, my quest to define the adored guest got structured within me, unleashing the potential connection between us. As for me, the guest knew the way to my soul and the language to communicate with it. This is what I concluded and wanted to convey the same to that one 'ADORED GUEST' of mine.

~ As in my belief, they truly deserve all the recognition I have made for them.

Having known the reason the ' individual' was holding back, I then had to inhibit myself from dwelling in the world of soulful connection—which I once thought to be ours together. The aching comfort I had chosen to be with was making my path dusty, and that's when I could finally unleash them from me. But having been able to connect through just shared thoughts, I could feel an intimacy that transcended physicality. For me, it was indeed a soulful connection.

Whether it was I who felt it all, or was it fate that connected me with a soulmate who felt the same, or was it all just an outcome of unintended actions coated with warmth to be just presentable – all remains unclear to this date… A while already, but I'm yet to confirm with my heart, which refuses to unsee whatever it saw while visiting the cornered space beneath the individuals soul. Having been left unreturned, yet again, I would fail to feel less rosy but act insane and look for the obscure possibility. Because the already offered roses were voluminous with the possibility that -

'We could be us together!'

By pouring my heart out, here I let my voice lament with an aching gravity—

WE COULD BE US T.O.G.E.T.H.E.R !

I sound insane—rightly !

Now that I have all the reasons—

to hold myself back,

cage my emotions,

and set you free from my world, which I used to consider OURS before...

Where we enjoyed the immense pleasure of

PLATONICITY- with just uttered words , and shared thoughts.

And in between those uttered words, and shared thoughts,

I would feel a sense of pure intimacy...!

That at times transcended physical proximity...

A soul's connection, I felt !

Do you not agree?

Years passed, and I'm still unclear about whatever it was between us, if not what I had intuited ?

In between receiving and still looking for—

My equations balanced and bore fruit.

But my weak boundaries let you in, again & again & again... every time...!

Even if there was a mere chance !

Unreciprocated—yet full of rosy energy !

As I was convinced with enough hope—

That you could be all mine !

So call me insane—ok, fine !

But I still imagine us t.o.g.e.t.h.e.r...!
~ unapologetic

16 Feb 24

A fondness that was seeded in my heart, left me with distorted ambiguity, and I couldn't help but count only the roses the individual offered me. While on one side, my adoration to be alongside them remains unrequited, I have failed to refrain from longing for their return on the other side.

With a heavy heart, as fate was crystallizing for me, I then yearned to express to you :

And, Like All Things Do,

I Know, You Too Will Pass One Day -

Far Away, Beyond My Reach !

Then, If We Meet Someday, Unplanned,

On The Roadside —

I Will Foresee Silence Only…

~ a Longing

20/2/24

MY UNREQUITED SURRENDER...

By now, you've explored the past whispers that have revealed the delicate threads of connection between me and the individual, along with my eventual longing for them. Now, as I guide you into 'My Unrequited Surrender,' you'll delve deeper into the realm where my hopes reach their limits and my surrender becomes a poignant reflection of my unfulfilled desires.

So, like all other things, the individual too passed on. No, it wasn't because I was unaware of their temporality, and so I had enjoyed visiting those spaces where they once visited. The reason I kept lingering there was that, somewhere, I failed to erase the baggage of hope that once stemmed from our seamless exchange of time.

And when light reflected on the pre-decided fact, I had no other way to carry them alongside, but to submit myself to the season, and entirely to the invisible reason, to which I had knotted my heart. While roses kept blooming in my garden of heaven where the GUEST had earlier visited, the contemporary sway of their transience made me wail the wishes that I had stored in for them—compelling me to ask for their apology.

Upon reflecting on the connection the individual and I shared in the later period, I found myself surrendering to fate—acknowledging the inevitable. The realisation of my submission to this unseen force mirrored back to me, like a truth I had long avoided. In this space, the language I use now embodies that unrequited surrender, a blend of seeded hopes that were once alive and the distorted echoes of those same hopes fading away. It is here, in this delicate balance of surrender and longing, that my words reside wherein:

- I pour out my journey with the impactful individual.

- I submit myself to their presence.

- I repent for not being able to let go of the connection.

- I justify my cause for having found a home in them .

- I long for their possible return.

- I describe their aura.

- I narrate the reasons that led me to define them as heaven when I was 21.

- I project the invisible reasons that invited me to settle in a home.

- I express how I felt the organic pull towards their being.

And at the end, I agonizingly pour out my core desires with a lamenting apology, surrendering to the depths of my heart.

The verses presented in sequence contains the elements of bittersweet surrender of my hopes that never fully received reciprocity from the individual. They capture the essence of my unreciprocated emotions and my silent resignation to the inevitable fate the individual held over me.

As you came across the first seasonal impact on me, where I couldn't help but fall, it was in the apricity of winter when we greeted each other evenly. You then showed how the rain swept everything away, leaving me dried up. Later, I had to fall like those leaves in autumn.

Having been left fallen, dried, and scattered, I somehow processed rejuvenation with the seasonal returns of the individual. Here, "season" is a metaphor for the individual's temporary visits, just as the seasons change. With each return, I consoled my soul with their fleeting warmth, akin to the winter's apricity. With such a fragile span together, I was once again left scattered when their inner storms pulled them away, leaving them no choice but to refrain from visiting me. They then chose to remain remote, iced, and out of my reach.

Even so, their coldness couldn't prevent me from lingering in those spaces where they seasonally visited. So again, I danced with the fleeting sway of the seasons before submitting myself to them.

SEASON AND I – SECOND

Your return alone was able to bring me measureless joy,

so was the reason,

every time I fell—

like those leaves in autumn...

But having left dried, and unsettled,

With passing time, I too faded...

Apricity then felt soothing,

but was temporary...

Very soon,

Splashes of monsoon left me all scattered, and disarranged.

Perhaps the reason,

Spring then turned into a distant

Ally !

I was all open to bloom,

but failed in reliving...

As it was there,

but was all iced and far !

Unable to break the ice,

I was left to linger—

In those spaces,

where you once inhabited...

18/4/24

Reality sank in, and I was left overwhelmed by the turmoil of emotional baggage I was loaded with. I could no longer live through the seasons, as they had forbidden me from participating—unlike before. Submitting myself was the only way I could see to resolve and dim the stubborn flame within. So, I began bottling up instead, as the more I lingered in the blank space of the room that was once a home, the more the flame would get heated over the reason of my submission. Also, the effect of the deep periodic sway of the individual was palpable. Hence, I shut the flame and submitted myself to not only the seasonal visit of the individual but to the entire reason for their visiting.

SUBMISSION...

It's been a while, since the obvious was revealed.

But I linger in the room—

that I once had access to.

Although it is remote now,

a part of me is still full of purpose.

As the roses I was offered with are yet on count...

But lately, I've started to bottle up

the whole of me :

All that I once felt , and exchanged.

As by now I know :

All of that was for a

'reason only'.

The periodic sway runs deep,

and the pre-decided fact has left me to submit.

Not to the season only,

but to the whole reason—

to which I had glued up my heart.

9/5/24

What do I do after my submission ? I can only repent.. Having known the cause of unbridgeable space with the individual, gave me all the reasons to repent over setting my heart on them, back the time when we had just greeted. Upon failing to convince my heart to accept the fate, it doesn't forbid, but continues to hold dearly, the hopes once seeded from our seamless exchange of conversations. Thus, it serves me as the source, which allows me to recall and treasure the bygone memories.

In this verse, 'Forbidden Heart', I do not repent over not being rational in my tender age; rather, the baggage of emotions that holds me back with an unattainable hope is what I repent over. The serendipity of events bore me a fruit that I could not have attained, possibly never in this given life. It wasn't a voluntary role of theirs to do so for me, yet I cannot stop myself from conveying my gratitude to them.

MY FORBIDDEN HEART...

Had I forbidden myself,

from setting my entire heart on you 'that day,'

I would have been able to withdraw myself from visiting those emotions 'today'…

Now, if you ask:

"What is visiting those emotions to me?"

I would simply say: it was home to me then,

but the truth weighs heavy now,

perhaps due to spaces...

It has fragmented all of the roses from my home...

Reason being so heavy !

Yet my heart remains in denial...

How do I even convince?

Little could I know about the revelation before,

I wouldn't have gotten totally into...

Perhaps I'm to be blamed for that "yesterday"...

But I'm not here, to just say:

What all could have happened, or prevented,

I'm neither here, to shoot you with all my rants.

Rather, to convey my warmest gratitude...

'Coz how everything fitted me so right that—

The impact you've had on me has showered me with infinite blessings, ones I could never have asked for on my own in this lifetime."

But things haven't been so at ease, right?

It's a story, I would someday narrate for sure...

9/5/24

Hereby, I make a narrative of how it felt to know the individual closely. With no other way before me but to submit myself to them, while my heart disagrees to let fate win over the other side—thus awakening the spirit within me that could connect with the individual.

The ' Home' resembles the ' individual ' here, with whom I could feel at home , whom I could hear beyond what they uttered. Their energy was warm enough to comfort me, and that all made me feel like a shower of magical aura over my tender heart. Not knowing to set limits, since I was tender at age, all I knew was to warp myself in whatever my heart could recognize as genuine. Their words were impulsive , yet I could sense the muted voice in it. The impact was so palpable that, even to this day, I involuntarily recall those bygone times and feel life in them. I hold on to the ambiguous possibility, but again, the fate weighs heavy, I then realize the void within - but at the end their energy wins in pulling me towards them…

THE HOME

The home I associated with, felt own to me,

I could hear the voice behind,

read beyond the narratives !

It was all perhaps the reason,

I could address my spirit to it.

A bud at the age to know and draw limits !

An unrefined stage:

All I knew was to look for solace and cocoon my heart.

Half-evolved, and raw, to be picky,

All I did was wrap myself in whatever I was offered.

The aura ! the impact !

—everything spoke volumes to me !

And what more could a bud needed ?

It was all beyond an answered prayer…

A miracle ! All magical !

My joy knew no bounds, knowing their words of validations as all for me…

Even to date, an involuntary recall holds enough life in it.

I float in the clouded sky,

While many other times, I walk in the void !

Yet again, I surrender to their gravity,

As their memories continue to drive me to the moon…

1/6/24

What do I do, but blame my heart ? For it will neither accept the fate that was unfolded, nor allow me to forbid myself from feeling life in the home where the aura of the individual can no longer be felt.

In the previous verse, you saw the emotional dissonance between my attempt to accept fate and my heart's refusal to do so, as it remains drawn to the home I was so fond of in my tender age.

This verse, however, reflects my inner voice, which, with an excited spirit, still counts on the possible return of the individual. It knows well that planning for a reunion with them is nothing more than an unattainable fantasy. Even so, my heart remains captivated by the warmth it once felt. Because the individual seemed so intimately my own that my heart stubbornly holds onto them, despite knowing they are beyond reach. It refuses to relinquish hope, no matter how impossible it may seem. As I was a bud at that age, I couldn't deny what I sensed; instead, I called them my home. Everything felt so fulfilling that they planted within me a hope that still resonates, irresistibly pulling me back towards them . This hope does not let me sit in stillness, but allows me to adore the serendipity they brought, accompanied by a melancholic weep.

AN UNCERTAIN POSSIBILITY...

Even today, the possibility of you to be here, excites me...!
While it's just a pie in the sky,

and that, I can only pan out

building castles in the air...

But I have been to the room :

Where, losing ourselves meant addressing both of our spirits,

and the warmth in your spirit would shelter me in a home,
which I could call mine !

With deep contentment,

I have found enough roses in the garden of that home -

to settle with the half-complete fantasy,

and embrace the blue, within the blues, in melancholy...

16/6/24

While grappling with the conflict between accepting fate and my heart's refusal to acknowledge that I could no longer visit the captivating place where the individual whom I once adored as a home resided, I was also enduring the void their presence left behind on the other side. Despite knowing they were gone, I clung to the memories of what I believed was unconditionally meant for me – their essence, their presence, which felt like home.

Reflecting on the time when I had access to them, and now being distanced from that connection, my heart treasures every moment we shared. The fondness they infused within me still lingers, and their complete, wholesome presence remains the only thing that draws my sight back to them.

Never had I ever witnessed such fondness in me for anyone before; it was their complete persona to whom I succumbed and developed an adoration that transcended mere fondness. The energy was so evident that, even after submitting myself and acknowledging fate, I couldn't resist, nor could I prevent my heart from confronting the void they left in me.

So then, I again positioned myself in the place once occupied by them. Knowing the fate and passing through the aftermath of it, I learned to contain my wails and refrain from complaining about their absence.

While living through such mental and emotional discord, both my mind and heart opened the lingering scar. Putting aside my efforts to hold my tears back, I couldn't restrain myself any longer ; the rock inside me started to crumble, and I wept... wept... and wept... knowing their inevitable void in me, and that they would never, ever visit me again…

After I was done addressing their forever adieu, I decided not to blame them, but instead to cherish the stroke of luck they involuntarily offered me.

A SPECTRUM OF EMOTIONS

The view I saw

While you were behind ,

was a spectrum of emotions—

All in a band, like a rainbow !

Even today, when I position myself there,

the rock inside me breaks out ,

 and recollects the long-gone period.

And unlike the past -

I do not wail !

Nor do I complain of your absence…

From sitting beside the bottom line

to on top of the moon—

My heart fluctuates.

And when the extremity of fluctuations hits the lowest,

the human inside me, laments for your presence...

But I wake up calm... !

And embrace the stroke of luck you have unwittingly given me-

One that has now become an infinite source of joy for me,

Wherefrom I could possibly never have enough...

17/6/24

Upon positioning myself in the space that the individual and I once occupied together, I could immerse in vivid emotions which had a lasting impact on me. The impact was so intense that, even after submitting myself to fate, I failed to entirely convince my innermost self that the individual had gone forever. I couldn't persuade myself that my inner child's friend, who had been my soul's solace, would no longer return to share their time. As time passed, I realized how tender I was, unable to help but wrap myself in the warmth the individual showered upon me. With this realization, I could also rationalize every moment I was drawn to them in the past. I understood that I had ample reasons to consider them as my heaven. Their energy was so compelling, their inner self was so generous, that I surrendered my spirit to them. No fortune could have promised me such a soul mate, nor could I have found one on my own.

It was through a serendipity of events that a path was paved to them—a path that illuminated the numb and gray corners of my soul. On this path, we could lose ourselves in each other so completely that even the weight of fate couldn't prevent me from revisiting those lived moments. Reflecting on these half-complete moments, I realized that perhaps 21 was too tender an age to have fully grasped the transient nature of the individual's visit. Thus, I defined them as my heaven.

PERHAPS A HEAVEN...?

Maybe

21 was too early

to define heaven.

It was then – when I felt the organic pull towards you...

It was then – when I could effortlessly address my spirit to you...

It was then – when I could entirely lose myself in you...

Nowhere could I ever feel myself -

so in detail,

so at home, and at peace !

A bright light's reflection -

to the grey corners of me.

I know, I cannot still wish for your solace

to last forever...

So, for the given time -

my echoes remain unheard !

my whims remain unanswered !

and my longing has turned into numbness... !

Yet, you remain the most precious encounter that life has ever granted me.

My inner child is unknown to what cannot be true.

It still questions me :

" When will I ever again visit my soul friend ?

There's so much I wish to share with them—thoughts and emotions that have grown over time. I yearn for the chance to reconnect and bridge the gap left by their absence."

I go numb…

And thus, it receives back no answer from me…

So perhaps the reason—

It remains in joy,

hoping you would visit again…

All these were my subjects

that defined heaven for me at 21.

5/6/24

What gravity the individual held that made me to call them my heaven when I was 21, you all know it by now, right ? If you have come across that, then may I trust you to additionally know that:

Even after, I could feel a heavenly energy in them,

Even after, we could find ourselves so detailed when we had loosened up, Even after, I felt complete, so complete that I believed they were destined to be my soulmate,

• they had an invisible reason, which they could never share, nor could I ever question. Blindfolded by hope, I refused to judge them; instead, I have always harbored an adoring thought, even about their invisible reasons. How could I not ? There were times when they involuntarily poured out their heart— a heart that was tired, starving to be listened to, not complaining, but invisibly weeping for all the warmth they have been deprived of due to an unrealized yearning . How could I even question them after witnessing all that tender corner of their heart ? I couldn't.

But I too am born with flesh and bone like them; I too needed to convince my heart, which is still in denial about accepting the fate that broke the bridge between us. My subconscious mind—who knows all the stormy moments I endured and has stored all the despair against the individual—knows that neither of us was wrong for the seamless exchange of time between us. It was an invisible reason they have held within, to which I perhaps was destined to meet.

Not with the intent to cause conflict, but I needed to provide my distressed mind with a space to narrate all my desolated resentments, irrespective of who would ever hear them, including the individual.

With a heart filled with adoration for them, along with the never-addressed discontentment that has simmered inside my head, here, in this verse, I have I reflected on them with a rational thought that - perhaps, I was too young to have responded, and contained my emotions . As I now have come to realize that –

no matter, how far I had sailed the boat together,

no matter, how many hours I have seamlessly shared with them,

no matter, how much trust I could build upon their genuine energy,

no matter, how safe I felt with them and no matter, how Inviting they appeared for me, I shouldn't have let myself invest my entire heart and spirit in them, prematurely. As latter only, did they crystallized the fact for me that I can never have access to their invisibility. So eventually, I realized that I will forever remain a guest in their story.

As a reflection on these underlying reasons, I then whispered to myself :

THE INVISIBLE REASON

I now know that—

You aren't supposed to settle in a home:

For the reason that you felt you belonged to them just as much as they felt you were theirs...

For the reason that you could feel their safe invitation...

For the reason that you could witness their transparency toward you...

For the reason that you could listen to their unuttered voice...

For the reason that you both could light the platonic fire without stint !

For the reason that you got undeniably connected to them !

For the reason that you got pulled toward them and became inextricably bound !

For the reason that you were vulnerably in conversation till dawn !

For the reason that even hours would shy away, upon watching you both surrendering to become one...

As everything was real, and so had you felt...

Also, their words were obscure and uneven –

not a lie, but not quite the truth either.

And so, for the reason, you remain only a guest to that home...!

28/6/24

MY SOAR THROUGH THE BLUES !

Having surrendered to fate, I needed to address the root of my feelings—a budding hope nurtured by the individual, whether intentionally or not. Yet, despite my submission, a persistent voice kept challenging me, resisting the idea that my innermost soul was misguided by them. Deep down, I knew that my feelings for the individual were genuine and not born of mere desperation. However, facing the reality of our situation, they made me question my instincts and dismiss my tender emotions.

The aftermath of abruptly encountering the reality, combined with the disregard I experienced right after, and my heartfelt beliefs, left me with an internal struggle. I grappled with the fact that my feelings for them were genuine, yet, whether due to my tender emotions or circumstances, I was forced to accept them as mere delusional fantasy. This turmoil ignited an unbearable flame within me, and I soared through the blues.

THE TENDER FALL

For two people to feel themselves belong to each other,

It is necessary for them to have known each other inside out.

And perhaps, that is a basic demand that seems unarguably true !

But what if I told you—my falling for you was organic ?

It was the first time I could witness your generous heart.

I then developed an admiration…

Definitely not right after we met,

but after we got to know each other better.

So much better that we felt an inextricable gravity towards each other,

which let us weave an unassailable thread of connection !

And upon building such a closeness,

My heart now refuses to unlearn what it felt for you.

It refuses to accept that our connections was unreal.

It refuses to erase :

Your name !

Your thoughts !

The baggage of your memory…

Allowing you to continue visiting there.

While it wails on the other side,

Knowing you are a guest only,

Yet it has repeatedly failed to prevent me

From giving you the space within.

Unclear to define—what strange spark had occurred in me…

which now denies to unlearn the mental proximity we shared…

My taste in dealing with emotions was somehow raw,

so was supposedly the reason, I have failed to be wise to you…

~ a fragile vessel to carry the weight of words…

29/6/24

The underlying cause that brought me to repent over my fateful encounter with the individual, also infused me with an unrelenting desire to paint my core wishes on a blank canvas, creating a space where they can be validated. As fate crystallized, I then realized that I could no longer sit with a distorted rose ; instead, I needed to convince my stubborn heart that this individual can never in this given eternity, share the rest of their time , nor can they create new moments with me, no matter how much they might wish to. My desires will therefore remain unrequited forever.

Thus, the verse "A Wish Half Perfect" reflects my desires: which resonate with the individual and have stemmed from the proximity we once shared – a connection that transcended mere physicality. However, fate's interruption displaced us, making them an unattainable pursuit for me. My wishes, which once had the potential to be realized together, have remained half-fulfilled, yet perfect, because, their verbal assurances were enough for me to know what their heart has stored in for me. So goes the title – "A Wish ~ half perfect".

Here, I not only convey my yearnings but also seek their apology : as my language might not fully fit their part due to foraging circumstances that have bound them to another. Because I believe that they do not deserve to be held accountable for all that I sensed from our seamless exchange of time, which is now a bygone story – one that was never meant to be, was an unrequited tale that ended before it began…

A WISH ~ HALF PERFECT...

I do not wish to hold you accountable for how it feels to be in,

knowing every second of a day—

that we can only see each other shooting ahead,

but can never meet...

As we both are now parallel to each other—

We are, who we are...!

And at no cost, we can be "US" together...

But I have a wish !

I have a wish : to make you sit beside me someday,

and let us again lose ourselves in a conversation, deeply...

A conversation of curiosity,

and a conversation of unimaginable compassion...

I have a wish : to wrap my arms around you,

and walk through a midnight street.

I have a wish : to make you listen to my unspoken narratives,

and let you know—

how intensely I could feel the pull towards you and

how deeply I had lost my heart on you...

I have a wish : To communicate with the invisible self of yours...

I have a wish :

To make you feel desired and adored in the way—

You have solemnly wished for...

I have a wish : To just be there for you.

So that, I can assure you of all your needs-

Not out of desire only,

but because you are worthy of it all.

I have a wish :

To wrap you in my embrace,

with the unwavering desire

I have treasured in my heart for you !

I have a wish : to offer my shoulder to you...

So that, when the child inside you would weep,

I can then be given the opportunity

to witness your inmost heart :

to be nourished...! and spoiled...!

with the sensual cocoon

you have always deeply longed for,

and find the ultimate solace for your ever deprived heart.

I have a wish : to just have you beside,

and complete our story…

> *~ i am sorry*

29/6/24

With the sequence of these verses, the ending of my tender experience is told, revealing the depths that led me to feel, fall, and eventually surrendering fully to the reality that our paths could not intertwine further.

Now, as I conclude my collection of verses from 'My Unrequited Surrender,' I find myself at the crossroads of acceptance and hope, enabling me to realize that this journey through surrender revealed not only the unhealed wounds of my unrequited desires but also the profound strength I've discovered in embracing my own vulnerability.

In this way, the ROOM, the SEASON, the GUEST, the HOME, the HEAVEN, and the SPECTRUM OF EMOTIONS—each symbolizing the 'individual' introduced in the section entitled Whispers of My Guiding Angel—and I had to come to terms with reality and heed the forces of fate, which led us to drift apart…

A FEW EXPLORATIONS INTO BEING HUMAN

A JOURNEY THROUGH TURMOIL AND REDEMPTION

As I navigated the final year of my bachelor's, I faced unprecedented challenges that tested my mental and emotional limits. This chapter recounts my journey through turmoil and redemption.

In the beginning, as the veil unfolded, you encountered hints of the inevitable storms I needed to navigate. Now that you've reached this point, I hope you are more familiar with the angelic individual with whom I had the fortune to interact and share a few platonic moments. Soulful moments like those I felt when I shared more of myself with them were invaluable for a budding spirit like me to cherish. However, I found myself caught in a spiral of emotional confusion. I had developed deep feelings for them, yet I had to come to terms with the reality that our connection could never evolve beyond a certain point. This truth became clear to me after they gently, but firmly, communicated that their life was shaped by other significant pursuits and responsibilities that took precedence. Despite this, our connection remained genuine; it was a bond we both acknowledged, though it could never be fully reciprocated in the way my heart longed for. We chose to step back, to maintain our distance, allowing the boundaries of respect and circumstance to guide us. I believe my interaction with them brought significant illumination to me, because their presence felt deeply meaningful—as if they were drawn into my experience and became a part of my journey.

However, the fate they revealed, led me through a period of turmoil—a harrowing time detailed in the section entitled "Whispers of My Guiding Angel: A Journey of Renewal and Transformation"—the individual's rational advice and support were crucial in helping me navigate immediate challenges and regain stability. With their help, alongside validation from my closest ones, I managed to piece together my almost shattered self and reengage with sanity.

Not all the dust settled, nor could I fully convince myself that I had been wrong in how I perceived them. I was trying to heal from the emotional heartache of unrequited affection— it was in that period itself my academic pressures showed up and added another layer of strain. The burden of both these emotional and mental struggles led me to a critical juncture. But being in the final days of my bachelor's, I had to act immediately and return back to my responsibilities and prepare for both finals and entrances. I realized I had two months (April and May) to get through both the exams. To be sincere, I didn't have the slightest confidence in myself, and I was intensely consumed by thoughts like "What if I don't make it?" "What will I do if I can't pursue higher studies?" These thoughts pushed me into a downward spiral, causing me to confront insecurities l had never faced before. I was aware of my incapability's, and so the irrational fear stemmed from my low self-confidence. But I had never in any of my worst nightmares thought that there resided such harmful demons inside me—demons that were impossible for me to escape, but had to confront.

To get control over them, I had neither enough rationality nor wisdom to safeguard myself. To clarify, the 'demons' I refer to symbolize the intense, irrational fears and self-doubt that overwhelmed me during this period. They represent the internal struggles and psychological turmoil that made it nearly impossible for me to maintain control over my thoughts and actions. These demons were not literal but rather a manifestation of my deep-seated anxieties and insecurities that seemed to consume me from within. Time dragged on, and managing my sick mind alongside the studies was the toughest task to deal with.

However, knowing the challenges of getting through my exams, I had to pull myself from the mental sickness and prepare a schedule to get ready at least for the finals. Believe it or not, after putting hours into preparation in those last months before the finals, I could evenly get through the markings. But those evils inside me hadn't shut down; instead, their energy felt so harsh that I began to act psychotically. I started panicking every second of the day. Every bit of my body began to lose control. Upon losing control over myself, I became prone to reacting to every other person I interacted with.

Even trustworthy friends in college, who had no idea of these thoughts, were met with my reactions to their words and actions. Eventually, there came a time when I completely slipped into the abyss dug by those demons inside me. What followed ? My insecurities reached their peak, and I felt tortured within my own body. Psychotic sensations heated me up, and I began to seek refuge—somewhere I could feel secure from all ends. So I travelled home, twice within a month, hoping that being with my family would help me get better. But all their consolations and my coping efforts went in vain.

The consequences of my unstable mental state were far-reaching. My exams neared, but due to the severe instability of my mind I couldn't battle with the psychotic fear of failing caused by the demons inside me. Day after day, I began to lose focus and totally dissolved into the coming time. I couldn't recall even the simplest of answers during my exams, including those I had previously prepared . My state was so erratic that I resorted to desperate measures, employing unauthorized methods during the exam, as I had no other way to cope. A decision that only added to my distress when they somehow discovered it, causing me overwhelming guilt. The repercussions were devastating, and at that moment, I had no option but to surrender myself to the overwhelming breakdown, watching helplessly as all these incidents unfolded.

It was during this period of severe mental degradation that something beyond my control happened: I began experiencing irrepressible and inexplicable physical urges within my body while inside the room I was living in. To this day, I remain unable to comprehend how this urge overpowered me, but it was impossible to resist, and I became entirely consumed by it. Despite my efforts to conceal it, they somehow discovered my struggles, though I was unaware of being observed. In response, they reacted with brutal harshness, unleashing threats and hurling degrading names, as if to strip me of my dignity even further. This public humiliation exacerbated my already fragile mental state, and

I felt utterly powerless, spiralling deeper into my psychotic breakdown.

No doubt I was in a sound place among those with whom I shared close familial ties, but during those challenging academic days of my bachelor's, they could offer no voice of assurance. Instead, they judged me in the worst possible way. Perhaps that was all they had stored for me since the time I was living with them.

I won't entirely conclude that, all of that they said against me was because they were cultured with a prejudiced mind. Instead, I would hold myself accountable for any of my behaviours that perhaps didn't fit soundly to them, although none of them were intended to target them in any way. On one side, I was battling to get through the ongoing exams, and on the other, they were actively shooting me with all the worst verbal swords they could. Such treatment caused me to negatively reflect on my past. From then on, I began to interlink past events. In many instances, I held myself accountable for behaviors I exhibited—likely because I was at a tender age and lacked the grace to respond, choosing instead to react. I harshly held myself accountable for all that I could recall as my bad deeds in the past, which was also an outcome of their mocking behavior towards me.

All in all, I couldn't find the safe shelter I was starving for. Instead, I ended up becoming the target of those with whom I was living. In the verses you will read—they encountered me with hostility and aggression, like those cops do. Yes, they even had that much poison stored against me. I admit that my behaviors during those days were unbearable for them, but my question is: Was it so unbearable for them that even after witnessing such odd and ill mental degradation of mine, they couldn't think that something might be wrong with me ? Could they not realize that, day after day, I was psychotically getting torn apart ? How could they backfire at me with their taunts, bullying, and even public encounters when I was already burning from the inside ? If those were their stored thoughts for me, then why did they treat me normally at face value and act as if they were my well-wishers? All these questions of mine remain unaddressed thus far. After I finished my final papers, I needed to immediately get myself out of there.

I came home, but who could drag me out from that abyss of my inner demons ? Who could stop me from reflecting negatively on my past actions ? No one ! Months passed, and every bit of my body began to survive death every second of the day. Having not prepared for entrances, I lacked the rationality to sit and start preparing. Each day, I was dying and trying either to harm myself or stop my breath…! As a result of repeatedly dwelling on certain, though not illusionary thoughts, I ventured beyond the reach of even professional help. With each passing hour, I was pulled by demons towards the burdened thoughts of bygone events. This torment persisted because I remained tethered to the past. I eventually realized the potential, albeit unintended, harm I may have caused to those I was connected with. But those realizations brought me no resolution. Instead, the more I connected with those bygone days, the more my psyche degraded. There were moments when I gave up on life. My family suffered with me throughout; they had no clue what I was going through, but they stood by me, holding me in their arms and arranging all the necessary aid they could. By September, my mother insisted on Enrolling me in a local institution to pursue a course. I resisted vehemently, shouting, "I have nothing left to go ahead in life! Why can't you understand that I will never succeed again?" Despite my repeated outbursts, she remained calm and continued to support me. I felt utterly hopeless, convinced that I had no future, and I tried to convince her that I wasn't deserving of her efforts. It was as though I was on the brink of giving up entirely, even attempting to prevent her from giving me a chance to rebuild myself because I didn't believe I could overcome my despair.

Over time, as I attended classes at the institution, the hopeful environment there helped me realize that it wasn't time itself that was harsh, but rather my own irrational thoughts that had occupied my mind. Those recurring thoughts weighed heavily on me each day, making me feel overwhelmed and unworthy. The kindness I encountered there—particularly from the teachers, who were unaware of my inner struggles—had an unintended yet profound influence on me. Their compassion, though not directed at my specific situation, helped me see the reality of my circumstances more clearly. They inspired me to recognize that it was up to me to navigate through my difficulties. Gradually, I began to climb out of the abyss of inner demons and break free from the cycle of negative thoughts. Not immediately, but eventually, by November, a day came when I deliberately decided to embrace hope, gather myself and march ahead. However, just as I was beginning to recover from this dark phase, a glimmer of hope emerged – something unexpected happened to me.

After months of silence, the individual reached out in response to something I had posted. Their message started with a straightforward check-in on my well-being, signaling a reconnection after our time apart. Our conversation was light and friendly, and we touched upon the personal struggles I had been working hard to overcome, which had caused me considerable difficulty. As we continued to talk, I sensed a subtle shift in the conversation.

They began to draw a parallel between my current situation and a pivotal moment in their own life. They shared something that profoundly impacted me, not just because of its content but because of the insight it offered into our connection. They revealed that they held me in high regard—so much so that they had mentioned our interactions to their important ones. They conveyed that while our connection was as deeply meaningful to them as it was to me, the circumstances prevented it from evolving further. They expressed that, under different conditions, they would have cherished the opportunity to nurture our bond.

Hearing these words from someone I deeply admired, especially after having gone through so much emotional turmoil, brought me solace. Their words thus held immense weight in me – it was like a gentle breeze during those tumultuous days, bringing solace and a glimmer of self-worth. It was a reminder that perhaps, in a different reality, our paths might have aligned. Their words ignited a transformative spark, lifted me from despair and infused my torment with a sense of hope and renewal. Not just because of what they said, but because of who they were—a person whose intelligence, resilience, and deep understanding of life shaped my perception of them. They had faced immense struggles in their own life, enduring significant hardships and growing up in a challenging environment, yet they remained someone with profound insights into people and relationships.

Their words were more than just a passing compliment. They validated the connection I had felt, confirming the depth of our bond. And while their circumstances meant that we could never be together in the way I once dreamed, their acknowledgment of my worth lifted me from my despair. For someone as perceptive as them to see me in such a light—especially when I had been doubting my own worth—gave me the strength to rise above the darkness I had been sinking into.

This acknowledgement, though bittersweet, was the catalyst I needed to rebuild myself. They reminded me that even in my lowest moments, I was valued, admired, and seen. That realization sparked the beginning of my healing, allowing me to escape the relentless cycle of hopelessness and mental degradation, discover the sense of self-worth that I had been desperately searching for, and emerge from the darkness to reclaim my life with a brighter future.

That subtle yet profound validation was like a balm to my bruised soul, one that resonates within me to this day and might continue until eternity. Although they were unaware of my struggles, their words provided profound support, helping me find strength and purpose in my darkest moments. This unintended validation from them thus illustrated the remarkable power of their impact.

It's because of this profound impact that I have expressed deep admiration for this individual in earlier pages.

As I continue on my journey of self-discovery, I've come to realize that understanding the linkages between my past behaviours and their consequences has been crucial in navigating the path toward my core self. Although memories of that tumultuous period still linger and causes painful flashbacks, I've learned to approach them with a newfound sense of self-awareness. The following pages contain subtle reflections of those memories, serving as a testament to my growth and resilience.

ADDRESSING THE INNER DEMONS

Life has confronted me with inner demons—
ones I neither had , nor could have imagined living with .
~ by birth, I suppose…

Overwhelmed by guilt,
I then threw myself into a clogged drain :
Where all the past floated, one event after another…
And each time,
It felt as if I was stung in multiple places.

I held myself accountable !
Judged myself harshly !
The more days passed,
The more prone to extremes
My mind and body became, reacting impulsively.
All beyond control: psychotic !
Perhaps, by then, I was too late for self-remedy…
As I had been consumed from the inside…

Incidents followed in succession !

None in my favor !

They confronted me instead…

Outsiders bullied !

Even the neighbors were no exception !

The bullying !

The loud spitting !

The incessant honking of four-wheelers—

All part of the torment unleashed against me

Remain undefined to this day…

What havoc in my head led to an outburst

Is a phenomenon in itself…

By then, I was already drowning…

Descending into the darkest depths of my mind !

Left with all the sins collected from the past,

A body of flesh and bone was all that remained…

May/2024

A SOCIAL CHAOS

They treated me normally at face

But applied all manner of nasty tricks—

To shatter my room of comfort -

And tear me apart entirely…

In the days that followed, they :

TAUNTED me !

MOCKED me !

BULLIED me !

THREATENED me !

And even after that wasn't enough,

At their worst !

They PUBLICLY HUMILIATED ME !

"How did that felt to me then?"

Or how those flashbacks still hit me like a train—

Remains untold to this day.

From losing my senses to nearly giving up on life,

I somehow survived death…

~ that's when I realized :

Knowing and living closely with someone is just a mere necessary, but not sufficient enough to cement a connection. Thus, our space remains uncertain and shallow in their story…

18/7/24

AN ACKNOWLEDGEMENT

Every other day, I would wake up with flashbacks of the same thoughts, which I had evaluated to be true, alongside successive events that further attacked my entire being. Having lost my sanctity, an imbalance of both mind and body caused me to descend into madness. Each panicked reaction of mine gave the bullies more ammunition to retaliate with prejudiced words and actions. Distorted and shredded from all ends, I couldn't prevent but succumbed to their abuse.

After enduring it all, my mind was consumed by flashbacks of illusionary thoughts and their suffocating actions. Each day felt like a struggle to survive, screaming for a death call...! I was so emptied that, even to say I had given up, I had nothing left !

I did have a circle of humble humans whom I could approach with a crying call, but during those time of such conflicts within myself, I could barley respond to any of their words of affirmations. There was not only one, but a couple of beautiful hearts, who offered me their empathetic ear, which I was starving for. Initially, I couldn't help myself even after receiving their kindest of consolations. But with time, patience, and continued support from these closest ones – particularly my mother, who assured me with her unwavering support, and a dear friend whose expertise in psychology was a beacon of hope, guiding me through the darkness with her insightful perspectives and gentle encouragement; she helped me reframe my thoughts, develop coping strategies, and foster a deeper understanding of myself. Additionally, my grandmother's limitless love, filled with wisdom and support, played a significant role in my healing. Their collective efforts helped me find the strength to rise above the chaos and sow seeds of hope in the face of tyranny.

Never will I ever be able to return their compassion, but I can only assure them of my deepest gratitude by bowing down to the most beautiful hearts they own.

Here is a little verse that narrates a day—when one amongst these angelic friends and I were in a room colored with lavender. Where she dressed me up in a red upper, upon dressing, she showered me with praises for my radiance. My soul, which had been consumed by darkness and had almost forgotten how to feel emotions, then felt uplifted and giggled with a joy I couldn't have realized by myself during that period of tough challenges.

This little verse is a celebration of her unshakable loyalty, trust, and confidence that she blesses me with -

In a room of LAVENDER,

My grey soul could feel the gravity of BLUE !

Guess what took me to feel so LIGHT?

She dressed me in RED,

and I could no longer stay upset—

But giggled with double the JOY !!

26/12/23

Reflecting on the vicious cycle of my setback journey right after the completion of my bachelor's in 2022, I realized how a year passed in the flash. Now, the setback wasn't entirely the issue that was holding me back from diving into academics with a resilient spirit. Rather, it was my self-doubt that pushed me into the drain of procrastination. I realized how I was developing irresponsible habits which, if not controlled or addressed, had the potential to degrade my future.

Consumed by overwhelming thoughts of self-doubt, I couldn't cultivate the confidence within, to take a stand and set an achievable target. Blessed with a supportive family who never imposed any pressure on me nor neglected my concerns, instead, they showered me with all possible opportunities to guide me through the challenges of time and assist me in securing a promising future. Even then, I remained stagnant despite being served opportunities and knowing the potential risks the challenges held. I couldn't easily escape the loop of procrastination. A year had already passed, and I was sitting passively, counting the time. It was during that time, these thoughts came forth from my inner self, and I couldn't restrict but noted them in my memoir as—

A SEATED YOUNG BLOOD !

The air is fresh, yet dusty !

Clear eyes, but vision is blurry !

A young blood seating passively,

Counting the sixteenth day of the first quarter !

But why ?

Why is a young blood seated ?

Why are you holding yourself back ?

Why, on this holy Earth, have you chosen to be just seated ?

Can't you appreciate everything that is served on your table ?

I know , you are well-aware of yourself !

You know it all –

How challenges effects you ! and

How to face every hindrance head-on with effective actions
!

But is that in any way serving you back ?

Don't you think it's a question of your worth ?

Don't you even realize that it's an alarm !

I have been watchful of how you let go of -

A minute !

An hour !

A day !

A week !

A month !

Alas, a year…!

It's the first quarter now, and ironically, you are passively
living -

With the same letting-go attitude !

But until when ?

See, you know -

How it feels to hit the lowest.

And now, when life seems to be on track (hopefully),

All set to climb the rocks,

It is disappointing to see you displaying and adapting all the potentially terrible habits…

Can't you see the peak, awaiting in silence, just for you to step there ?

I know the rocks will be hard on you,

But you have to unfold your sleeves !

Put on your boots ! and get back on track !

And in the days when self-doubt holds you back,

Try recalling the days –

When you stood up bold !

Those days, when you would be seated for hours on your chair -

With all your focus and sincerity, to make the most out of your time, in the most righteous way possible !

Recall -

How confident you were in yourself ?

Try recalling -

how it felt when your hard work bore fruit !

Eventualities are unpredictable -

There will be tests !

After test, after test, and after test !

Also, the inner demons… Huh !

They will sink in , uninvited, and

 trigger the subconscious.

You might then, end up a day, thinking of a nightmare !

And a night might feel shortened, thinking of a day mare !

And possibly, this might not be the end !

At times, the track might take you to an ocean—

Full of tides and waves !

But you have to be your own steady lighthouse—

To guide yourself throughout the voyage !

Who knows ? You might end up discovering—

Maybe the rock-solid route to your DESTINATION !

January 16, 2024

Never could I ever know how it feels to live on after death wins in taking away our most prized possessions until this year – 2024 when my grandma's breath stopped forever…

Losing her was my biggest fear since when I could realize how much she stood for me, as equally as if I were a part of her. But again, I owed no angelic power to have saved her from becoming mortal. Unready for such a fate to arrive so suddenly, I was then lamenting beside her paralyzed body… It was only in that moment of time , my heart could somehow address grief… I then wailed ! wailed ! and wailed… ! until she gave up on her breath.

So, upon addressing grief and acknowledging that death is unpredictably inescapable – which awaits us all…! And that, all that we think we own, they all are just to assist us in sustaining here in, until death wins over… - two of the verses I could phrase to visualize this realization are narrated beneath –

The initial verse conveys the idea that - we are all ordinary and that death is a shared fate. Meanwhile, the next idea presents that everything we possess is for temporary use, as time ultimately surpasses us in the race. It also suggests that we are all accountable for our actions, which lead to consequences that, in turn, become our individually threaded narratives.

TRANSIENCY

A running blood needs—

Little of assets:

To buy us clothes for protection,

Build us a home for shelter,

At least a few hearts to support

the process of enduring life with hope.

But until when ?

Until when is it in our hands to guard ourselves ?

The blood that is running will halt !

Flesh will stiffen and turn cold !

Everything will automate…

And we are no any wonder to escape,

But an ordinary home-

paving our way to the house of ashes…!

3/7/24

THING OF TRANSIENCY...

On weaving the past :

While the thoughts are being expressed,

the words remain undressed -

Letting it wear every new garment,

that each passerby would choose for its fit.

As it is certain :

That time will win over !

That years will succumb into a 'yesterday'

And 'you' and 'I' cannot help !

But resign ourselves—

To the hate,

To the love,

To the affection,

To the connection,

To the new beginning,

To the end of anything ! But time…

To the knowing,

To the known,

To the learning,

To the unlearning,

To see that cannot be unseen,

To every other 'thing of transiency'

We all choose to guard ourselves with.

"Who do you think?"

"Who offers us with?"

"By the self?"

Or would you agree with the traditional notion of

"Life offers us with?"

6/8/24

Upon reflecting on the behavioral differences we exhibit individually or in social settings, and by connecting this to some of my personal experiences, I realized that uniqueness lies within us all. We either adjust to or adapt ourselves according to these differences. It's the choices or circumstances we face that shape our 'made self.' While some may choose to be wholeheartedly authentic, others might struggle to reveal their true selves beyond their 'made self'.

With this idea,

I have tried to convey here that how we release our impressions on each other, which eventually impacts our lives - both 'supportively' and 'destructively'.

EITHER OF THE MIND OR HEART

They say:

"You are being addressed with their mind and not their heart."

The past me wouldn't have been positive about it.

But the time I'm in, is showing me that—

From and being at heart is hardly possible for some,

While being the complete opposite

For those who have cultured themselves to live on the surface level.

Endless possibilities show up

As to justify the cause of their being.

But if we can weigh the same for our bio physique,

If we can feel the same emotion while being in the same situation,

If we can frame our minds into wearing a lie,

If we can perfect the art of shielding ourselves with an inner tuff shell,

that we hardly remain recognizable.

Can we not put a little more effort to unlearn the negative ?

Can we not make a little adjustment with the switch of invisibility ?

Can we not just be rational with the fact that-

neither of us is carrying anything to our graveyards?

15/7/24

MASKED ~ A HABIT !

I heard about the "mask culture"

Then I witnessed the "in-person pretensions"

To some extent,

All those "masks" and "pretensions"

Might have reasons of their own.

But how does one justify the "habit of pretensions"?

Justify? It would take a goddess within for that.

—Preferable ?

In a given situation, there's an opportunity to be 'authentic.'

I guess one misses out on that, so it's lost eventually.

Now, I need not hammer my worth -

To justify this "masked habit".

~ Unapologetic, for all who choose authenticity !

17/5/24

I FAILED !

The more I am attaining the majority,

the more the sight of the bane of others

is becoming mirrored to me.

Recalling the bygone time—

When , at times, I stood hard,

while many other times, I reacted with prejudice

to those who needed just to be simply understood…

A sense of deep regret shoots through me…!

And I feel awfully apologetic to them…

I wish I were a little more heedful to have—

assured them the inner comfort they needed…

Had I had a complete heart,

I would have been able to be at least a shoulder for them to lean on,

when they were sobbing their hearts out.

The inner comfort of being heard,

when they were invisibly lamenting in the void…!

The need for unrefined validation,

the sense of being seen—

when they were dampened by the turmoil of obscurity…!

That's all they needed from me…

when they were reducing themselves to tears…

- but I failed…

9/7/24

A REPENTANCE

~ *My introspective self drove me back to the time, and somehow, I could realize that :*

Sometime before:

when my baggage of issues would overpower my identity,

while stepping into almost every new door that was opened for me,

it was then, a combination of self-doubt and embarrassment would pull me down and I would remain settled with the less…

Sometime before :

When I thought I was cautious enough,

In today's time, I realize that those thoughts and actions,

driven by the deep -seated fear inside me,

all reflected a darker part of me…

To which, I could have never possibly addressed myself.

Sometime before :

when I thought I was correct without a sin ;

the present me has identified all of my missteps,

 and thus refuses to agree.

Sometime before :

when I was trying to conceal my irrational fear of being left out ;

in today's time, I define them as my innate insecurities !

Sometime before:

when I thought I was at my best in sharing a company ;

today, I realize my faults, that might have possibly hurt so many !

Sometime before :

when I thought I was doing enough ;

today, I realize that I was barely empathetic.

Sometime before :

When I thought it was the other side who were wrong ;

Today, I recall how I was impulsively reactive to their actions…

Sometime before :

when I believed I could never be immoral ;

my recent past actions have defined how my blood can turn to boil…

Sometime before :

when I thought I was defining how love feels ;

the present me is of the equation that:

unconditional essence exists nowhere…!

But perhaps in the lap of our parents…

The rest all commit to the idea of transaction only…!

17/7/24

Apart from these elements, I have added a few lines to depict the kind of treatment received by those who are considered inferior, specifically by GENDER – in some corners of the world where patriarchal shadows loom. With that being addressed, I have aimed to bring forth some social parameters that has played a key role in shaping certain prejudices within the echoes of a social setting.

AGAIN...?!

Their shrapnel-like yells reveal –

How empty and discontent they are ?!

How uncivilized they are ?!

How much rust they contain ?!

How ethically hollow they are   ?!

How brooded their roots are ?!

How CULTURALLY STUBBORN they are ?!

With how much rigidity they have been raised ?!

For they will never mistakenly , ever, leave the head seat,

As they believe, they are born to fit in it.

Neither will they ever try to crack out from the cemented notions they are blooded with.

But,

How much longer will you let them pierce your peace ?

How many more moments will you allow their fury to sear your soul ?

How many more times will you keep your lingering scar hidden ?

Will they ever try to silence their rage ?

Will your scars ever be noticed by them ?

Will they ever know the depth of the torment they cause you, every time they throw theirs yells at you ?

Have they ever tried to ponder your silence? Or Will they even try ?

This is where you are tethered !

Perhaps they call it fate…?

Neither of you will ever be able to instill any mere amount of justice for you, if you settle for this 'CULTURED FATE'

If that is to be your side role,

Then you would never be able to set yourself free …

Instead, you will be succumbed into the loop of

"TABOOS"

16/8/24

RECIPROCITY THAT LEADS !

The opening unfolded with me narrating:

'Reciprocity that leads!' — a truth I have witnessed and a belief I have established over time. Now, as I proceed towards enclosing my pen, I am hopeful that you have followed the unfolding narrative, observing the radiance of those closest to me and even the peripherals who had the power to instill solace in me.

I hope you have seen how their collective assurances aided me in forging my own path and how I eventually overcame everything that was excruciatingly distressing and unclear. Yet, this journey is not mine alone. Through the narratives in the later part of this debut collection, I have explored reflections on diverse human behaviours, drawing from various social interactions to illuminate the ways we all influence and are influenced—highlighting the interconnectedness of our experiences.

These reflections, captured in the poems that delve into our shared humanity, introspection, and the complexities of human behaviour, illustrate how our actions and reactions contribute to a greater tapestry of understanding and growth.

Having read them, you may have observed how I have emerged 'UNINHIBITEDLY' through their reciprocated actions towards me. Thus, the reciprocated actions I received from them have been pivotal in guiding me through those moments of turmoil and even to this day.

AFTERWORDS

So, in the beginning, I shared a sprinkle of events that collectively became my threaded narrative, structuring a path towards self-exploration. Delving deeper, I discovered my affinity for the world of words. From then on, I have always invested myself into pouring my soul to weave my emotions. "Weaving Emotions: A Journey To Self – exploration" is the outcome of my ardent love affair with language. Never had I ever thought I'd have an interest in writing, but life's experiences, people, and introspection led me to discover my purpose.

As I reflect on my journey, I've identified key factors that aided my learning process:

1. **Introspection:** From aiding me to address myself with my inner voice, my core, my strength, and my weaknesses, introspection made me realize what drives me (considering both the positive and negative aspects) and what I need to unlearn in order to construct my vision and purpose.

2. **Accountability:** To your belief, initially I wasn't able to easily digest these insights. However, encountering life's events led me to embrace active introspection, enabling me to held myself accountable for my own patterns of behaviours. By doing so, I could navigate the root of whatever circumstantial eventualities

I dealt with, together with embracing the resilient spirit within me.

3. **Self-awareness:** Through active introspection and accountability, I was able to renovate a space for my entire existence, ultimately leading me to connect myself with the circuit that wires me.

4. **Need for Emotional validation:** Many times, I found myself overwhelmed by emotional turmoil while surviving through the ambiguous phase, where, I both thrived and struggled to an unimaginable extent. I was totally raw and lacked knowledge of the world outside, which made it difficult to act in a rational manner. However, with the unwavering support and guidance of those who believed in me, even when I had lost all faith in life and in myself, their positive presence sheltered my damaged soul and profoundly influenced me. Their heartfelt reassurance gave me the strength to develop resilience, to make room for all my emotions—both negative and positive—and to validate them, rather than rejecting shamefully .

Through writing, I've found that conversation stems from knowledge and ideas, and it is the structuring of words into meaningful sentences, that resonate deeply back and forth with readers. For me, writing establishes a connection with who reads, allowing them to engage on a deeper level, which then guides them towards certain values – that are beyond any moral lesson. Also, I firmly believe that authentic communication is about heart-to-heart connection, which I've aimed to emphasize in my expression throughout the pages.

Furthermore, sharing our hearts is essential for genuine communication – don't you agree?

Dear reader out there, my heart this side goes beyond mere words to express my gratitude towards you for spending your valuable time in listening to my echoes. I feel truly blessed to have you and look forward to sharing more narratives in the future. As we part ways, may our encounter be able to help you seed new aspirations in your journey towards self-discovery. I hope you honour your voice and heart , and allow yourself to take the lead in this journey to finding your purpose. May you develop trust, and believe that you will be guided by your own

'SELF ' in the best possible way, towards your destination!

Signing off with my deepest gratitude.

~ Uninhibitedly yours

12/9/24

Email- anuninhibitedsapient@gmail.com

Instagram - _inksofmyechoes

Thank You !